Fiddle Time Joggers

a first book of very easy pieces for violin

Kathy and David Blackwell

Illustrations by Martin Remphry

T0071135

Welcome to the Third Edition of **Fiddle Time Joggers**. You'll find:

- open string pieces and tunes using the finger pattern 0–1–23–4
- duets—start with the staves marked ☆; come back and play the other part later!
- three new pieces, replacing nos. 3, 29, and 44
- audio play-along and backing (accompaniment only) tracks available to download from www.oup.com/ftjoggers3e or to access on principal streaming platforms
- audio practice tracks (recorded at a slower tempo) for some pieces, also for downloading/streaming
- piano and violin accompaniments available separately in printed collections
- An ideal book to use alongside *Fiddle Time Starters*
- a book for violin that's also compatible with *Viola Time Joggers*

OXFORD
UNIVERSITY PRESS

Great Clarendon Street, Oxford OX2 6DP, England

This collection © Oxford University Press 1998, 2001, 2005, 2013, and 2022
Unless marked otherwise, all pieces (music and words) are by Kathy and David Blackwell and are © Oxford University Press. All traditional pieces are arranged by Kathy and David Blackwell and are © Oxford University Press. Unauthorized arrangement or photocopying of this copyright material is ILLEGAL.

Kathy and David Blackwell have asserted their right under the Copyright, Designs and Patents Act, 1988, to be identified as the Composers of this Work.

ISBN: 978-0-19-355940-0

Music and text origination by Julia Bovee.
Printed in Great Britain

Contents

Open strings **3**
1. Bow down, O Belinda (*duet*) 4
2. Under arrest! 4
3. Someone plucks, someone bows (*duet*) 5
4. Down up 5
5. Two in a boat (*duet*) 6
6. London Bridge (*duet*) 6
7. Fast lane 7
8. In flight 7
9. Lift off! 8
10. Katie's waltz 8

First finger **9**
11. Copy cat (*duet*) 10
12. Tap dancer 11
13. Rhythm fever 11
14. Here it comes! 12
15. So there! 12
16. Rowing boat 13
17. Ally bally (*duet*) 13
18. Tiptoe, boo! 14
19. Travellin' slow 14
20. Lazy cowboy 14

Second finger **15**
21. Off to Paris (*duet*) 15
22. Clare's song 16
23. City lights 16
24. The three friends (*duet*) 17
25. Peace garden 17
26. Summer sun 18
27. Phoebe in her petticoat (*duet*) 18
28. Ready, steady, go now! 19
29. Cooking in the kitchen (*duet*) 19
30. Happy go lucky 20
31. The mocking bird (*duet*) 21

Third and fourth fingers **22**
32. Algy met a bear (*duet*) 22
33. Listen to the rhythm 23
34. Cattle ranch blues 24
35. In the groove 24
36. Stamping dance 25
37. Distant bells 25
38. Lazy scale 26
39. The old castle 26
40. Rocking horse 27
41. Patrick's reel 27
42. Calypso time 28
43. Knock, knock! 28
44. Rocky mountain (*duet*) 29
45. Carrion crow (*duet*) 30
46. Flying high 30
47. Fiddle Time 31

Music Fact-Finder Page **32**

Open strings
G
D
A
E
crotchet
(quarter-note)
crotchet rest
(quarter-note rest)
minim
(half-note)
minim rest
(half-note rest)
dotted minim
(dotted half-note)
whole bar rest
(whole measure rest)

1 Bow down, O Belinda

American folk tune

2 Under arrest!

Count 2 bars

KB & DB

Say the word '*rest*' quietly to yourself as you play.

3 Someone plucks, someone bows

Traditional
Words KB & DB

4 Down up

Count 2 bars

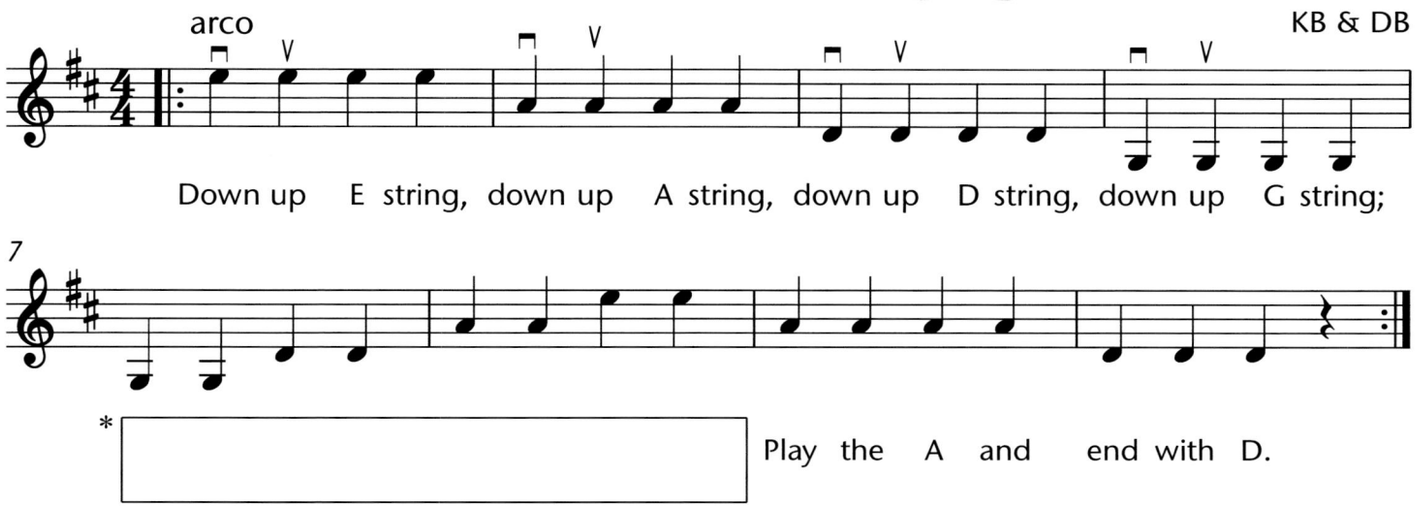

* Fill in the letter names of these notes.

5 Two in a boat

American folk tune

6 London Bridge

English folk tune

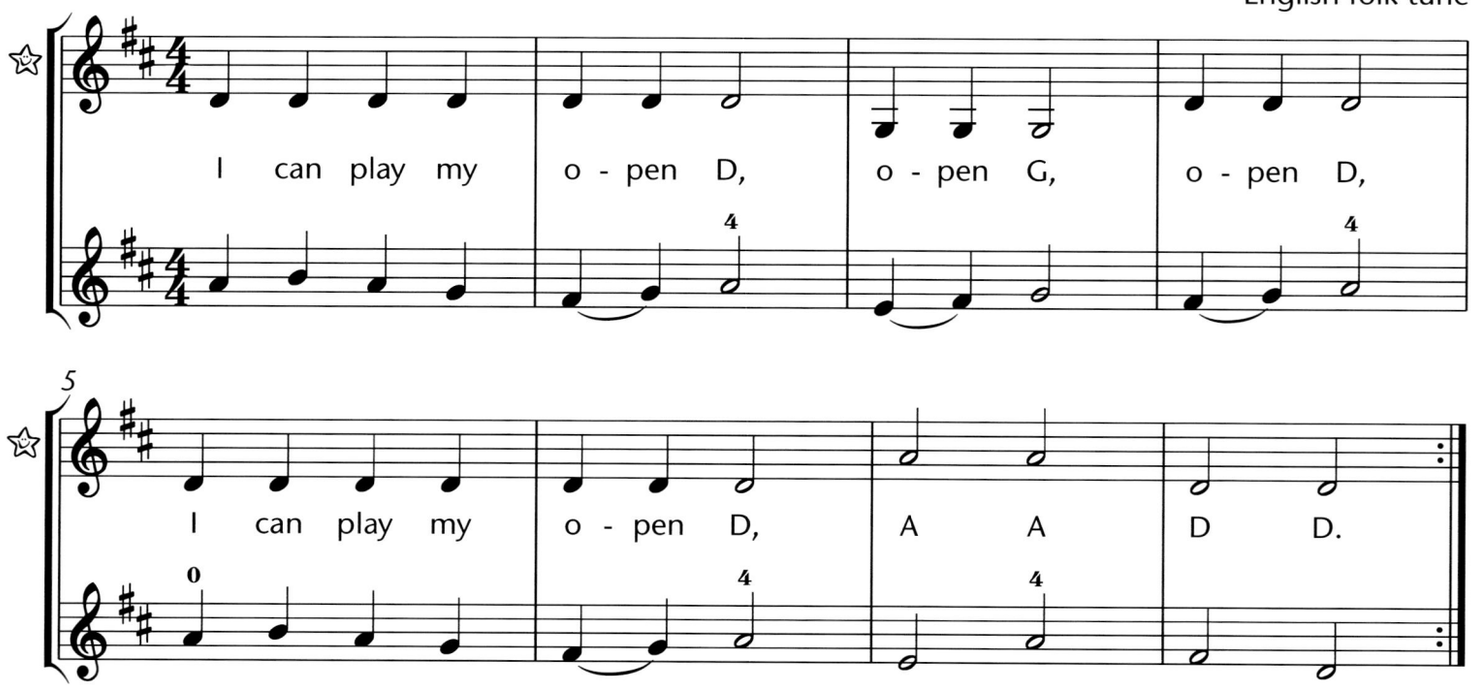

7 Fast lane

Count 2 bars

KB & DB

Fast

Try even faster the second time through!

48 Practice tempo

8 In flight

Count 4 bars

KB & DB

Calmly

In the rests, let your bow make a circle as you swoop and soar like a bird.

9 Lift off!

KB & DB

Rock

5

9

1.

2.

Lift your bow off in each of the rests and let it orbit! (Make a circle with your right arm.)

Try playing this rhythm variation in each bar:

Or - bit round the moon. (*etc.*)

10 Katie's waltz

Count 4 bars

KB & DB

Gently

13

1st finger
0
1
G
A
0
1
D
E
0
1
A
B
0
1
E
F#
semibreve
(whole-note)
semibreve rest
(whole-note rest)

11 Copy cat

KB & DB

1

D D E E

Can you play what I play? D D E E

5

Fine

Can you play what I play? Play it now with me.

9

1

A A B B

Can you play what I play? A A B B

13

D.C. al Fine

Can you play what I play? Play it now with me.

12 Tap dancer

Count 2 bars

KB & DB

Steadily

* Hold the bow upright and tap the screw end of the bow on your music stand.

13 Rhythm fever

Count 2 bars

KB & DB

Rock tempo

49 Practice tempo

14 Here it comes!

KB & DB

* Think of a foody rhythm and play it on these notes.

Here is an idea to start you off:

15 So there!

Count 4 bars

KB & DB

16 Rowing boat

KB & DB

17 Ally bally

Scottish folk tune

18 Tiptoe, boo!

Count 2 bars

KB & DB

Spookily!

Tip-toe tip-toe tip-toe, boo! (*etc.*)

Boo! (shout!)

Also try playing this pizzicato.

19 Travellin' slow

KB & DB

In first gear

20 Lazy cowboy

Count 2 bars

KB & DB

At a gentle trot

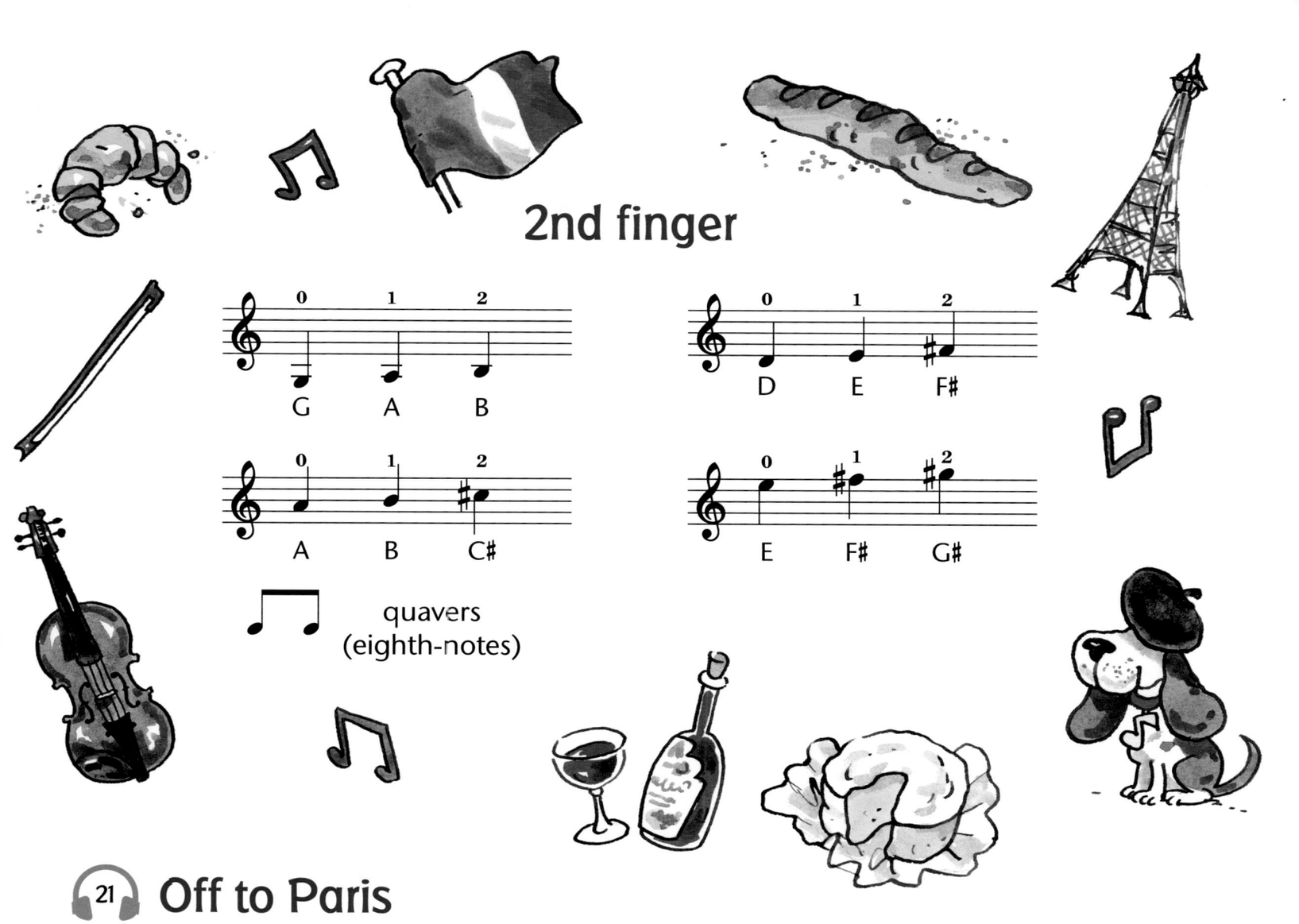

21 Off to Paris

French folk tune

22 Clare's song

Count 4 bars

KB & DB

Gently

mp

13

21

mp

29

rit.

p

23 City lights

KB & DB

Gutsy

f

5

9

mp

mf

13

f

24 The three friends

Finnish folk tune

25 Peace garden

KB & DB

26 Summer sun

Count 4 bars

KB & DB

Gently

mp

mf

mp

dim.

p

From now on, you'll be able to play both parts of the duets.

27 Phoebe in her petticoat

American folk tune

mf

mf

Swap parts when you do the repeat.

Practice tempo

Cooking in the kitchen

KB & DB

pizz.

mf

pizz.

mf

5

arco

arco

9

f

f

30 Happy go lucky (for Iain)

Count 4 bars

KB & DB

Sunnily

f

11

mf

17

f

23

29

ff

31 The mocking bird

American folk tune

Gently like a lullaby

mp

mp

5

8

11

rit.

Now you can play the harder part of 'Someone plucks, someone bows' on page 5.

32 Algy met a bear

KB & DB
Words anon.

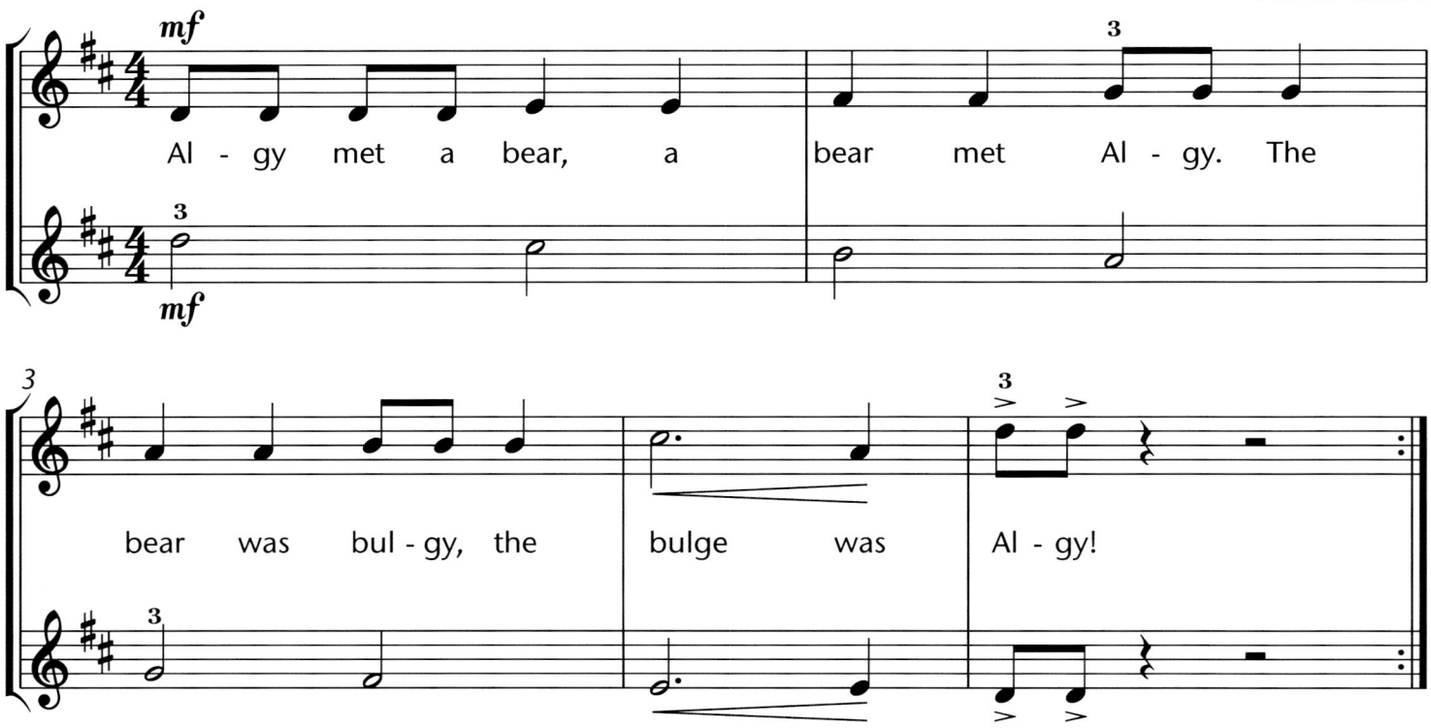

Swap parts when you do the repeat.

33 Listen to the rhythm

Count 4 bars

KB & DB

f 3

Lis - ten to the rhy - thm on my vi - o - lin. Crot-chets sound like
Quar - ter - notes like

10

this: Crot-chets sound like that!
this: Quar - ter - notes like that!

15

3

Lis - ten to the rhy - thm on my vi - o - lin. Mi - nims sound like
Half-notes sound like

20

this: Mi - nims sound like that!
this: Half-notes sound like that!

25

Lis - ten to the rhy - thm on my vi - o - lin. Se - mi - breves like
Whole-notes sound like

30

this: Se - mi - breves like that!
this: Whole-notes sound like that!

51 Practice tempo

34 Cattle ranch blues

Count 2 bars

35 In the groove

Count 2 bars

Now go back to page 15 and play the harder part of 'Off to Paris'.

36 Stamping dance

Czech folk tune

Try the harder part of
'Bow down, O Belinda' on page 4.

37 Distant bells

Count 2 bars

KB & DB

38 Lazy scale

39 The old castle

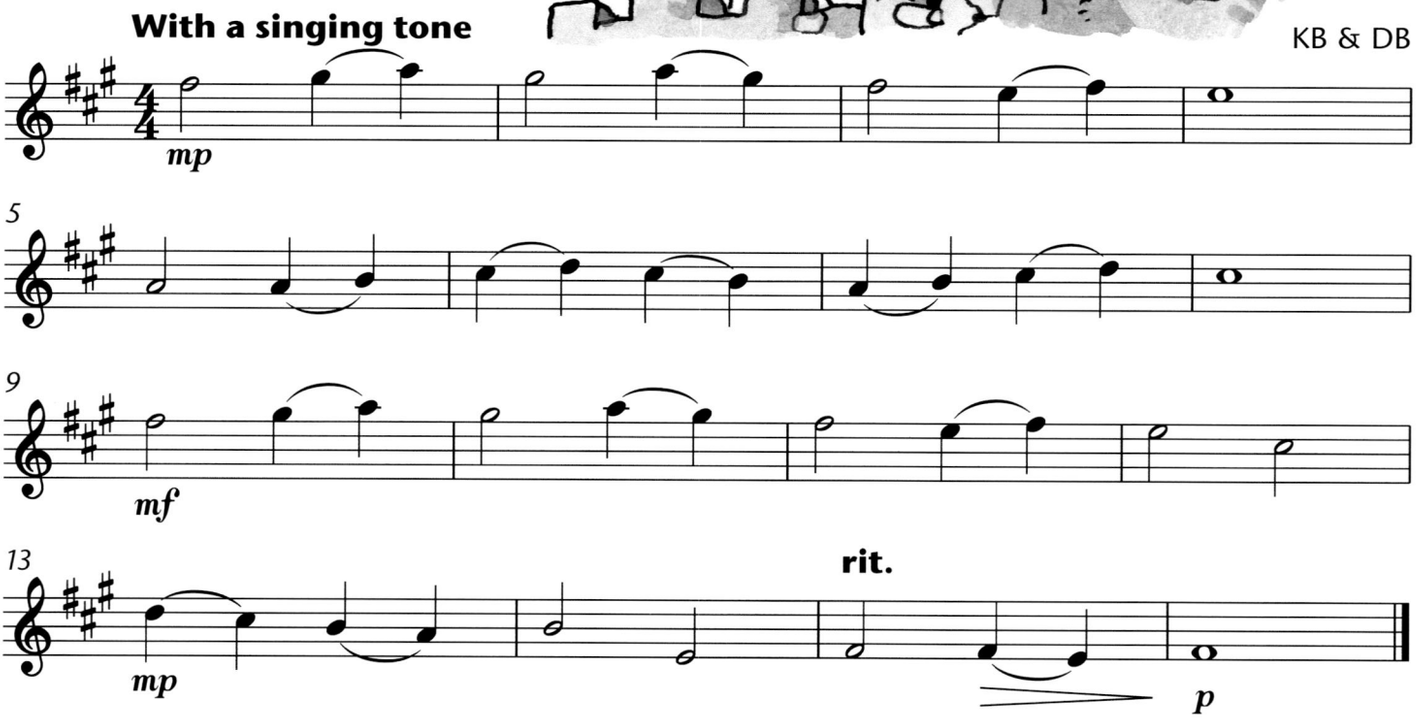

Now go back to page 16 and play 'Clare's song', slurring three crotchets (quarter-notes) to a bow.

40 Rocking horse

Count 4 bars

KB & DB

Gently

mp

11

17

1.

2.

rit.

Fine

21

mf

25

D.𝄋 al Fine

41 Patrick's reel

Count 2 bars

KB & DB

Energetically

mf (repeat *p*)

7

(*cresc.* on repeat)

Fine

11

f

15

D.𝄋 al Fine

52 Practice tempo

42 Calypso time

Count 6 bars

Carnival tempo

KB & DB

mf

11

15

cresc.

f

20

1.

2.

pizz.

mp

Now go back to page 13 and play the harder part of 'Ally bally'.

43 Knock, knock!

Jokingly!

KB & DB

f

'Knock, knock.' 'Who's there?' 'Cook.' 'Cook who?' 'That's the first cuc-koo I've

4

heard this year!' 'Knock, knock.' 'Who's there?' 'Jes - ter.' 'Jes - ter who?'

7

'Jes-ter min-ute, I'll un - lock the door!'

ff

Make up some other 'Knock, knock' jokes and play them on your violin.

44 Rocky mountain

American folk tune

Now try the harder part of 'Copy cat' on page 10.

45 Carrion crow

American folk tune

Brightly

f (repeat *p*)

f (repeat *p*)

5 4

f

f

p

p

9

mf

mf

rit.

Try the harder part of 'Two in a boat' and 'London Bridge' on page 6.

46 Flying high

Count 2 bars

KB & DB

Smoothly

mp

7

11

mf

f

15

rit.

mp

p

Try the harder part of 'The three friends' on page 17.

47 Fiddle Time

Count 4 bars

Easy going
𝄋 (a tempo)

KB & DB

f

9

13

17

1.

2.

pizz. **Fine**

21

mp

25

cresc.

mf

rit.

D.𝄋 al Fine

53 Practice tempo

Music Fact-Finder Page

Here are some of the words and signs you will find in some of your pieces!

How to play it

pizzicato or pizz. = pluck
arco = with the bow
⊓ = down bow
V = up bow
> = accent
𝅘𝅥𝅯𝅘𝅥𝅯𝅘𝅥𝅯𝅘𝅥𝅯 = tremolo

Don't get lost!

‖: :‖ = repeat marks

|1. | |2. | = first and second time bars

D.C. al Fine = repeat from the beginning and stop at **Fine**
D.𝄋. al Fine = repeat from the sign 𝄋 and stop at **Fine**
rit. = gradually getting slower
a tempo = back to the first speed
𝄐 = pause

Volume control

p (*piano*) = quiet
mp (*mezzo-piano*) = moderately quiet
mf (*mezzo-forte*) = moderately loud
f (*forte*) = loud
ff (*fortissimo*) = very loud
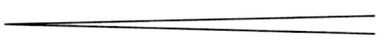 or *crescendo* (*cresc.*) = getting gradually louder
 or *diminuendo* (*dim.*) = getting gradually quieter

Audio credits
Violins: Ros Stephen, Catrin Win Morgan, Marianne Haynes; *Viola*: Felix Tanner; *Cello*: Laura Anstee; *Piano*: David Blackwell, Julian Rowlands; *Drums and percussion*: Andrew Tween; *Accordion*: Pete Rosser; *Guitars*: Kevin Byrne, Dan Thomas; *Trumpet*: David Geoghegan; *Clarinet*: Nicola Baigent; *Flute*: Marta Goncalves; *Voice*: Lin Marsh. *Engineers*: Ken Blair, Michael Taylor, Jeff Spencer, Ros Stephen; *Programmer*: Edmund Jolliffe